Parent
☆ ☆
Police

☆☆☆☆☆☆☆☆☆☆☆☆☆☆☆☆☆☆☆☆☆

THE U.N. WANTS YOUR CHILDREN

☆☆☆☆☆☆☆☆☆☆☆☆☆☆☆☆☆☆☆☆☆

by Ingrid J. Guzman

The Salt Series

Whether it's as salt of the Earth,
or salt in the wounds, Christians are to be the
element that distinctly alters and flavors the
nature of the culture. The Huntington House
Salt Series is an accumulation of booklets,
addressing important societal issues, giving
encouragement to believers to persevere
without growing weary, and inspiring readers
to a deeper, truer walk with God.

Huntington House Publishers
P.O. Box 53788
Lafayette, Louisiana 70505

Library of Congress Card Catalog Number
95-75886
ISBN 1-56384-092-8

Printed in Colombia

Preface

For years, a handful of Christian thinkers and writers have been warning evangelical parents that the secular-humanist education apparat should be abandoned. There is no neutrality, they insist. There is no such thing as neutral education. It's never a question of *whether* religion should be allowed in public schools, it's always a question of which one, they say. The religion of choice today is secular humanism.

The majority of Christian parents look on such warnings with amusement and send their young children off to be taught by the God-hating state. "They're learning to be salt and light," they assure us.

But, all is not well for these parents. With the recent federal power grab known as Goals 2000, some parents are growing uneasy. Computer tracking systems, assessment testing, and intrusive questions on values and beliefs have parents attending boisterous school board meetings on Outcome-Based Education. "They have no right to invade our families' privacy!" parents cry. The amusement over the warning about state education is being replaced with alarm. The alarm is long overdue, because this same "neutral" state education system is now providing the framework for the ultimate program to annihilate parental authority. This program is known as the United Nations Convention on the Rights of the Child, and it is being promoted by child liberationists in the education realm. Its significance far surpasses the inevitable federal control of education. If this treaty is ratified, parents will be up against the United Nations. A recent public service announcement of the United Nations International Children's Emergency Fund (UNICEF) contained the slogan, "UNICEF, because every child is our child." We'll see.

Whose Children?

At the heart of the debate over education, public standards of decency, and the state of popular culture is one foundational question: To whom do the children belong? The Word of God teaches that children are gifts, given by the Lord, for which parents and parents alone are ultimately responsible for educating and raising. The Scriptures are filled with references to God's view of children, and guidelines for proper care of those children.

> Lo, children are an heritage of the Lord: and the fruit of the womb is his reward. As arrows are in the hand of a mighty man; so are children of the youth. Happy is the man that hath his quiver full of them; they shall not be ashamed, but they shall speak with the enemies in the gate. (Ps. 127:3-5)

Nowhere in this verse, or in any verse in Scripture, is there found an expression such as "it takes a whole community to raise a child." Nowhere is there mention of the role of the state in advocating for the child's "inherent rights." There is no talk about a child's right to "self-determination" in Scripture. The Bible does, however, make clear the proper chain of command in households when Colossians 3:20 says, "Children, obey your parents in all things: for this is well pleasing unto the Lord."

Not only do the Scriptures teach the responsibility and ultimate authority of parents in matters of child-rearing, but hundreds of years of Western legal tradition also favor parental rights. Doug Phillips of the legal staff of the Home School Legal Defense Association points out that a landmark Supreme Court Decision, *Parham v. J.R.* (442 U.S. 584 [1979]) gave an extremely strong statement of parents' rights to control the important decisions which govern their minor children. Writing for the majority, Chief Justice Burger made this comment:

> Our jurisprudence history has reflected Western civilization concepts of the family as a unit with broad parental authority over minor children. Our cases have consistently followed that course. . . . The law's concept of the family rests on a presumption that parents possess what a child lacks in maturity, experience, and capacity for judgement required for making life's difficult decisions. More important, historically, it has been recognized that the natural bonds of affection lead parents to act in the best interests of their children. [1 W. Blackstone, Commentaries 447; 2 J. Kent, Commentaries on American Law 190]

As with so many other legal presumptions, experience and reality may rebut what the law accepts as a starting point; the incidence of child neglect and abuse cases attests to this. That some parents "may at times be acting against the interests of their children" creates a basis for caution, but it is hardly a reason to discard wholesale those pages of human experience that teach that parents generally do act in the child's best interest. . . . The statist notion that government power should supersede parental authority in all cases because some parents abuse and neglect children is repugnant to American tradition.[1]

Other Supreme Court decisions have prohibited excessive regulation of the family and asserted the primacy of parental rights. In *Pierce v. Society of Sisters* (268 U.S. 510 [1925]), the Court said,

The fundamental theory of liberty upon which all governments in this Union repose excludes any power of the state to standardize its children by forcing them to accept instruction from public teachers only. The child is not a mere creature of the state; those who nurture and direct his destiny have the right, coupled with the high duty, to recognize and prepare him for additional obligations.[2]

The modern children's rights movement and the United Nations Convention on the Rights of the Child seek to undo not only the

Christian world view on child-rearing, but also long standing Western legal tradition.

Children's Rights:
The Beginnings

The idea of children's rights is nothing new. But, it was first put on paper in 1923. Nigel Cantwell, director of Programs for Defense of Children International in Geneva, points out that 1923 formally began the movement we recognize today.

> In that year, the council of Save the Children International Union adopted a five-point declaration of the Rights of the Child, setting out basic child welfare and protection principles, which became known as the Declaration of Geneva. The following year, the Assembly of the League of Nations passed a resolution endorsing this declaration and invited its members to follow its principles. In 1948, the newly constituted United Nations adopted a slightly expanded version containing seven principles. The United Nations General Assembly, on 20 November, 1959, promulgated a ten-point declaration, which served as the springboard for the CRC and is still valid today.[3]

It was in 1989 that the United Nations Commission on Human Rights adopted the U.N. Convention on the Rights of the Child, in the words of the *U.N. Chronicle*, "giving children's rights the force of international law." Nation

after nation began to ratify this treaty, agreeing
to comply with its laws.

While the history of this new international
treaty can be traced back to the turn of the
century, the extra fuel needed by the engines of
social change was provided by the sixties coun-
terculture revolution in the West. It was here
that an already warped ideology found cheerleaders among American psychologists. For
children's rights proponents, it was exactly what
was needed to move their agenda to the next
phase.

Children's Rights v.
Parents' Rights

In 1974, a book was published that was
supposed to herald a new era in the discussion of
children's rights. Psychologist Richard Farson,
co-founder of the Western Behavioral Sciences
Institute in La Jolla, California, wrote *Birthrights:
A Bill of Rights for Children.* Radical education
guru Dr. Carl Rogers said, "Farson has a compel-
ling vision—a movement for the liberation of
children."[4] It is a vision that is on the verge of
being fulfilled. In his ground-breaking *Birthrights*, Farson says:

> Child advocates now fall into two obvi-
> ously related groups whose goals both
> overlap and conflict: on the one hand
> there are those who are interested in
> protecting children, and on the other
> those who are interested in protecting
> children's rights. The first, motivated by

a concern for the basic helplessness of children, rely heavily on adult intervention in situations which victimize children. . . . This group of advocates, by far the largest, is responsible for a remarkable amount of protective legislation for children and for making visible many of the ways in which children are abused and victimized. . . . The second group of advocates believes that ultimately children will be most helped not by continual intervention to protect them, but by work to secure their basic rights of citizenship. Believing strongly in the potential of children to act for themselves, their interests lean more toward liberation than protection. Their commitment to freedom for children is a strongly ideological one deriving historically from Rousseau through John Dewey and more recently Paul Goodman, Carl Rogers, A. S. Neill and Wilhelm Reich.[5]

The first category Farson refers to would include those who make laws relating to child abuse and mistreatment of children that mirror similar laws for adults, something most everyone would agree is needed. The second category is another matter altogether. The "children's rights" advocates have more in mind than protecting children from physical harm. The agenda is a radical one, and it is gaining ground. Richard Farson falls into the latter category, his presupposition being that parents are little more than biological incubators for completely autonomous, if undersized, human beings. The crusading Farson sets this forth in his chapter entitled "The Right To Alternative Home Environments."

> As parents now perceive the situation, it is their fundamental rights to have children and to raise them as they see fit. The 1970 White House Conference on Children, however, offered a different view. The conference held that the rights of parents cannot infringe upon the rights of children. As a society we may soon come to a similar conclusion, that *the ability to conceive a child gives one no right to raise that child,* and that raising a child gives one no right to dominate or abuse him. *The decisions about a child's home environment should not belong to his parents alone.* The child must have some rights to choose also. And if he is too young to choose, his rights must be protected by having an advocate acting in his behalf. (emphasis added)[6]

While Farson's views on allowing children to have full access to sexual freedom, pornography, contraception, jobs, the voting booth and just about anything else their little hearts desire, may sound extreme, it is important to realize that he is one of many "advocates" for children who have written that children should be allowed near complete autonomy, with the state providing assistance in establishing and maintaining their "rights." The views of these advocates have laid the foundation for what is coming.

John Holt, author of another seventies assault against the family entitled *Escape from Childhood*, writes:

> I urge that the law grant and guarantee to the young the freedom that it now grants to adults. . . . This means, in turn, that the law will take action *against* anyone who interferes with the young people's right to do such things.[7]

In the same essay he further states,

> What we can and should do is leave to the child the right to decide how good his home seems to be and give him the right if he does not like it to choose something else. The state may decide to provide or help provide some of these other choices. . . . It should give the child the right to say no to it as well as to his parents.[8]

Richard Farson lays out his views on what a children's bill of rights should look like.

1. The right to self-determination
2. The right to alternative home environments
3. The right to responsive design
4. The right to information
5. The right to educate oneself
6. The right to freedom from physical punishment
7. The right to sexual freedom
8. The right to economic power
9. The right to political power
10. The right to justice

Twenty years after Mr. Farson's and Mr. Holt's books were written, we are seeing their vision realized. Something that looks hauntingly like Richard Farson's Bill of Rights for Children is about to be ratified as an international treaty in the United States through the United Nations Convention on the Rights of the Child. The questions that concerned parents need to ask are: From where is the notion derived that children belong to the parents, to raise, to teach and educate? Do children have the right to self-determination? If not, why? How much authority are you as a parent prepared to cede to the government in deciding these questions? And lastly, what will the consequences be for your child and for the church of Jesus Christ, if there is a law passed granting your children the afore-mentioned bill of rights?

The U.N. Convention on the Rights of the Child (UNCRC)

Child-rights activists have failed to pass the radical legislation they want to see in place in America. What the government has not done, however, may now be done by the newly revitalized United Nations in one enormous step through something called the U.N. Convention on the Rights of the Child. According to the National Center for Home Education, the precursor to this treaty, SR70, is in the Senate Foreign Relations Committee. As of the printing of this book, it is quietly and steadily gaining votes. After much debate, this treaty was finally put together in 1988 and for the first time creates a comprehensive charter advancing the agenda of the children's "liberation" movement:

> In *Missouri v. Holland,* the Supreme Court held that a treaty made by the President with the required concurrence of two-thirds of the Senate is, under the Supremacy Clause of Article VI, Section 2, part of the supreme law which takes precedent over contrary state laws. Thus, the U.N. Convention would constitute legally binding law in all 50 states.[9]

If this treaty is ratified, children would be granted rights which would be legally enforceable, through the use of a United Nations panel of experts.

What would the convention do? The following is a breakdown of the treaty's articles, written by Doug Phillips of the National Center for Home Education.

The Convention Would Give Children the Right to Disregard Parental Authority

Although several of the treaty's provisions offer generally positive, non-offensive platitudes, a substantial portion of this charter undermines parental rights. The U.N. convention would:

> 1. Transfer parental rights and responsibilities to the state.
>
> 2. Undermine the family by vesting children with various fundamental rights which advance notions of the child's autonomy and freedom from parental guidance.

3. Establish bureaucracies and institutions of a national and international nature designed to promote ideas proclaimed in the Charter of the United Nations and to investigate and prosecute parents who violate their children's rights.

The State Will Determine the Child's Best Interest

ARTICLE 3: In all actions concerning children, the courts, social service workers, and bureaucrats are empowered to regulate families based on their subjective determination of the "best interest of the child." This article shifts responsibility of parental judgment and decision making from the family to the state (and ultimately the United Nations).

The Provisions of the Treaty Must Be Enforced

ARTICLE 4: This provision makes clear that the treaty is not just a positive affirmation. Signatory nations are bound to "undertake all appropriate legislative, administrative and other measures for the implementation of the rights" articulated in the convention. In fact, the United States would be required to "undertake measures to the maximum extent of available resources ... within the framework of international cooperation in order to restructure society in accordance with the implementation of these rights."

All Children Must Be Registered

ARTICLE 7: In order to insure State and U.N. control over their development, all children must be immediately registered after birth.

Severe Limitations Are Placed on the Parents' Right to Direct and Train Their Children

ARTICLE 13: Under this provision, parents could be subject to prosecution for any attempt to prevent their children from interacting with material they deemed unacceptable. Children are vested with a "freedom of expression" right which is virtually absolute. No allowance is made for parental guidance. Section one declares a child's right to "seek, receive, and impart information and ideas of all kinds, regardless of frontiers, either orally, in writing, or in print, in the form of art, or through any other media of the child's choice."

ARTICLE 14: Children are guaranteed "freedom of thought, conscience and religion." Children have a legal right to object to all religious training. Alternatively, children may assert their right against parental objection to participate in occult, Muslim or Buddhist worship services.

ARTICLE 15: This article declares "the right of the child to freedom of association." If this measure were to be taken seriously, parents could be prevented from forbidding their child to associate with people deemed to be objectionable companions. Under Article 15, children could claim a "fundamental right" to join gangs, cults, and racist organizations over parental objection. Parental rights and responsibilities are unmentioned.

The Convention Would Further Entrench the Right of Teenagers to Abort Their Babies

The convention is not only vague but contradictory when it comes to the critical issue of the right to life of an unborn child. Although some might argue that the language of Article 6 would favor the rights of unborn children, neither abortion nor unborn children are specifically mentioned. That provision reads, "stated parties recognize that every child has the inherent right to life."

The fact that several of the signatory nations not only permit, but as a matter of state policy actively encourage, abortions among its citizenry lends further credibility to the view that this is not a prolife measure. Article 16 states that any positive benefits resulting from the language of Article 6 are clearly undermined by the "right to privacy" purportedly granted to children under Article 16. Although the United States Constitution nowhere grants a woman the right to abort her baby, "privacy" was the operative word used by the Court in *Roe v. Wade* to create the right to abortion. This United Nations sanctioned "privacy" would seemingly establish as "the law of the land" the child's right to obtain an abortion without parental notice, the right to purchase and use contraceptives, the right to heterosexual and homosexual promiscuity, and the right to pornography in the home.

(Note: remember how extreme Richard Farson sounded when he said that children should have the right to all material, even that which may be deemed inappropriate? With Senate ratification, this will become the supreme law of our land.)

The State Must Assist in the Raising of Children

ARTICLE 18: This provision not only encourages two-income families by granting children a fundamental right to state subsidized, state-run child-care facilities, but it calls on the state to be co-parent by rendering "appropriate assistance to parents and legal guardians in the performance of their child-rearing responsibilities and shall insure the development of institutions, facilities and services for the care of children."

Parents Who Don't Comply Will Be Prosecuted

This provision mandates the creation of an intensive bureaucracy for the purpose of identification, reporting, referral, investigation, treatment, and follow-up of parents who, in violation of the child's "rights," treat their children negligently.

A Prohibition on Corporal Punishment

ARTICLE 28: Education is declared a "right" which is not only to be universally free, but compulsory. This section would require that the United States pass laws and develop an infrastructure geared toward "encouraging" all school-age Americans to be part of the school system. The nations of the world are challenged to unite in the creation of an internationalist approach to education. Finally, parties to the convention must ensure that school discipline is administered in a manner consistent with the child's human dignity as defined by the United Nations. Presumably, this would prohibit corporal punishment.

Education for the New World Order

ARTICLE 29: It is the goal of the state to direct the education of the people it governs toward the philosophy of the New World Order as "enshrined in the charter of the United Nations." Each child must be prepared to be a responsible citizen by having "the spirit of understanding, peace, toleration, equity of sexes, and friendship (for) all peoples, ethnic, national, and religious groups of indigenous origin," including, presumably, cultic, anti-Christian religions, and those regimes which embody authoritarianism and intolerance.

International Experts Will
Parent Our Children

ARTICLE 43: An international committee of ten "experts" is to be established to oversee the progress of the implementation of this treaty.[10]

* * * * *

The U.N. Convention on the Rights of the Child is being hailed by child's rights activists as the harbinger of a new era for children. Stuart

Hart, of the Office for the Study of the Psychological Rights of the Child, Indiana University-Purdue University at Indianapolis, writes:

> The recently adopted UN Convention on the Rights of the Child (UN General Assembly, 1989), covering a broad range of categories (e.g., health, family, education, maltreatment, freedom), is the best available formal expression of international opinion on the rights of children. It has the status of a legally binding international treaty for all nations that ratify it, now that more than twenty nations have done so. The UN Convention on the Rights of the Child is a strong indicator of the increased, formal, societal emphasis being given to participation and autonomy or *self-determination rights for children, in balance with protection and nurturance rights.* Nearly one fourth of the substantive articles are participation and self-determination rights, assuring access to information, freedom of movement, association, belief, expression, privacy, liberty, and development toward independence. The Convention's adoption is the formal beginning of what may be the most important period yet for advancing children's rights. (emphasis added)[11]

What Dr. Hart is saying is exactly what alarmed Christian leaders are only now beginning to realize. The U.N. convention poses a grave threat to parents who believe that children are not the property of the state, but a gift to parents by God. In other words, Christian parents are on a collision course with the secular, transnational state that is emerging.

Dr. Hart even predicts that conflict *will* ensue if the U.N. convention is ratified in this country.

> Children's rights more definitely focused on the self-determination issues of access to information (Articles 13 and 17) and the holding and expression of personal beliefs (Articles 12, 13, and 14) present their own problems. These principles, played against the convention's respect for the rights and duties of parents to provide direction and guidance for the child (Articles 5 and 14), *predict conflict between parental authority and children's rights.*(emphasis added)[12]

Dr. Hart has misspoken. These principles predict conflict between parental authority and the *authority of the state*.

A Positive Ideology of the Child

Dr. Hart's lengthy article in the January 1991 issue of the *American Psychologist* speaks of the challenge to psychology that the children's rights issues represent. What does psychology need to provide?

> Public opinion, policies and laws are converging in support of assuring self-determination rights for children to validate their person status. To do so responsibly, an appropriate balance be-

tween protection and self-determination rights must be achieved for children at every point in their development. To determine and support this balance will require the existence of a) empirical evidence of need and readiness for various protection and self-determination opportunities throughout the developmental period, b) a broadly supported positive ideology of the child, and c) the active involvement of children in establishing their needs and rights.[13]

Dr. Hart concludes this paragraph by saying that the U.N. Convention on the Rights of the Child is a "viable candidate for the *positive ideology of the child* to guide progress in children's rights during the next few decades" (emphasis added).

This article goes on to state that psychology can provide the empirical evidence needed to promote the ideas of self-determination for children. The bottom line of this thinking? Psychology is now being touted as the best way to provide "authoritative proof" of the self-determination needs of the child. All such people need now are a few studies that prove the negative impact a fundamentalist Christian parent has on a child, and the state can vote on the future of that child. *A little empirical evidence goes a long way in international court.*

Enforcement

How will the U.N. convention be enforced if ratified by the U.S. Senate? Author Michael Jupp writes:

John Williams, Director of Information at UNICEF has stressed that, even with the passage of the convention, "children will not benefit from these rights unless we as adults work for them." Williams emphasized the need to involve *the press in monitoring violations of the rights of the child, and to probe deeper and look for the acts of omission* . . . that probably kill and maim more children each day than the acts of commission. (emphasis added)

Michael Jupp concludes by saying,

Organizations are already mobilizing public opinion to generate the *political will for implementation*; activists are also developing monitoring systems to ensure that standards set in theory by the convention will be respected in practice by subscribing governments. (emphasis added)[14]

If the U.N. convention is ratified by the United States Senate, it will take precedence over United States law. If children are already in a public school, enforcement and monitoring of children's rights becomes relatively easy. The role of social workers and teachers simply expands to ensure that the children under their care are not having their "rights to self-determination" violated. The computerization of student records and the use of assessment testing could enable every school to keep close tabs on each and every student.

In order to enforce the United Nations Convention on the Rights of the Child, education of the general public will be necessary. Children will be targeted for education regarding their "rights to self-determination" and provided with the necessary course of action in the event that they perceive a violation of these rights has taken place.

The educators' publication, *Social Education,* devoted an entire special edition to the topic of the United Nations convention and how to integrate the teaching of rights into social studies curricula. In the words of William Fernekes in the lead article, teaching children's rights in the social studies class is a "critical imperative."

> Including the study of children's rights within the social studies curriculum as a major aspect of instruction in public policy and public issues appears both logical and essential to the development of a self-critical, participatory citizenry. Because it would certainly serve as a means of assisting young people in realizing their potential as civic learners, the examination of children's rights should occur in social studies classes.[15]

Mr. Fernekes' apparent desire to help young people realize their potential in the area of civics sounds noble. But, further on in his article, he gets more specific about the reason students must be educated on the U.N. Convention on the Rights of the Child: "Letting young people examine the rights afforded them under the convention, and the manner in which they may be realized, permits the linking of concerns directly affecting young people with policies that are relevant to the entire society."[16]

The classroom makes a convenient pulpit from which to teach the new international creed of the autonomous child. Mr. Fernekes goes on to suggest that "it makes sense to permit young people to challenge the structures of authority and governance in their schools by using the rights in the convention as a starting point for policy deliberation."

But, how could the treaty be enforced in a nation that has a large number of private parochial schools as well as homeschools? And, how could the rights of small children be ensured when they do not come in contact with the state? The answer may be the Parents As Teachers program, pioneered in the state of Missouri. This program places state social service agents in the homes of families with small children. These agents are supposed to make notes on each visit, detailing anything that might put children "at risk." The potential uses of this system for monitoring violations of children's rights are endless. The framework is already in place in many states.

Teachers will be instrumental in informing children of their rights. Beverly Edmonds, teacher and executive director of Peace and Human Rights in Education in Berkeley, California, writes,

> Geraldine Van Bueren, who relates education with the increasing autonomy of the child, and Per Miljeteig-Olssen, who gives examples of children exercising their rights, offer interpretation and

guidelines for the participatory rights, and Ellen Moore's Amnesty International Urgent Action letters provide the teacher with a practical way to involve children in exercising their rights.[17]

To translate the edu-speak, Beverly Edmonds is suggesting here that several radicals in the international education business can show teachers creative ways to indoctrinate their children regarding their right to self-determination.

"Psychological Recovery" and "Social Re-integration"

The CRC is being hailed as a "progressive" document on children's rights because it includes terminology not found in earlier child's rights documents. One such progressive element assures "participation rights" for children. Nigel Cantwell points out that for the first time governments would have to allow children to participate in the process of government. Also, Cantwell points to Article 39 of the CRC as evidence of the progressive nature of this document. This section deals with children who have suffered various forms of "cruelty and exploitation."

Under the terms of Article 39, governments must undertake to promote these children's physical and psychological recovery and their social re-integration. This is a remarkable step forward, as is another of the convention's innovations: the obligation of governments to take measures to abolish traditional practices harmful to children's health.[18]

The questions should come thick and fast from those who know firsthand the dangers of vague terminology in laws. What constitutes "cruelty and exploitation"? To which traditional practices is the U.N. referring? What comprises health? Could any of this be construed to mean, for example, that a Christian parent is committing an act of psychological cruelty in telling his child about a literal hell, sin, etc.?

Will the church under the treaty be required to end this kind of teaching if the panel of ten experts sitting somewhere in Geneva decides this sort of theology is not in the "best interest of the child"? Isn't the term "best interest of the child" by definition highly subjective? And finally, what will constitute psychological recovery for such "abused" children? What exactly is meant by "re-integration"?

On 2 September 1990, the convention on the rights of the child came into force. By that time, twenty foreign states had already ratified it. The panel of ten experts was formed in 1991 by those states who signed on to the treaty. These are the experts who are to oversee the compliance of this treaty by those countries which have signed.[19]

The Potential, Practical Applications of the CRC

The potential harm from the application of the CRC in America cannot be overstated. Geraldine Van Bueren, director of the Program of International Rights of the Child at Queen

Mary and Westfield College in London, cheerfully writes about the annihilation of parental authority by the transnational state.

> Although the wishes of children and their parents often coincide, children may at times have an independent interest in education. For example, a child may wish to attend sex education classes despite the moral objections of his or her parents. International human rights tribunals must consider (1) whether children have the right to participate in decisions concerning the type of education they receive, and (2) what rights, if any, children have under international law if they disagree with their parents' choices.[20]

Van Bueren, a few paragraphs down, goes on to cite a case in Denmark that went to the European Commission of Human Rights where a parent did not want his child to attend compulsory sex education classes. "Commissioner Kellberg stated, 'It is hardly conceivable that the drafters would have intended to give parents dictatorial powers over the education of their children.' " He concluded that it would "be wrong for children who hold philosophical convictions different from their parents to abide by their decisions."[21]

For those who would insist that human rights commissions only worry about prisoners of conscience rotting away in Turkish prisons, the following question must be asked: What business does the state have encroaching on the rights of parents to keep their children out of sex education classes?

For those with any doubt about the CRC proponents' view of parents, Ms. Van Bueren makes the CRC's position perfectly clear. Under a paragraph heading that reads, "The Evolving Awareness of the Autonomy of the Child," she says,

> Until recently, this evolving awareness has been reflected only in minority opinions. . . . In contrast with general human rights treaties, the CRC does not incorporate a provision reflecting the parents' right to have their children's education conform to their (the parents') convictions. Rather, according to the CRC, children are entitled to have their own religious and philosophical convictions respected by the state.[22]

If this treaty is ratified by the United States Senate, parents all over the nation, regardless of religious creed or beliefs, will lose their right to raise their children as they see fit. The child's ultimate right to freedom of religion will supersede the parents' rights to teach their children. The child's rights will be backed by force of international law.

Threats to Homeschooling

The UNCRC poses several specific threats to the homeschool movement. According to Doug Philips at the Home School Legal Defense Association, Article 3, Section 1 of the treaty is one of the greater threats posed to homeschoolers.[23] This article states:

> In all actions concerning children, whether undertaken by public or private social welfare institutions, courts of law, administrative authorities or legislative bodies, the best interest of the child shall be a primary consideration.[24]

Phillips points out that the "best interest of the child" is wholly subjective. Traditionally, the entry point for the government in family matters is initiated by divorce—the breaking up of a family or a juvenile justice case where a crime has been committed. When there has been no predicate finding of family failure, and no criminal action on the part of the child, the state has no legitimate cause to intrude on decisions concerning child-rearing.

To those who scoff at the concept of undue state intervention under the UNCRC, Phillips recalls that the state of Virginia had its involuntary sterilization law upheld by the Supreme Court in 1927 in *Buck v. Bell*. He cites the words of Justice Oliver Wendell Holmes in delivering the 9–1 majority opinion.

> It is better for the world if, instead of waiting to execute degenerate offspring for crime or to let them starve for their imbecility, society can prevent those who are manifestly unfit from continuing their kind. The principle that sustains compulsory vaccination is broad enough to cover cutting the Fallopian tubes.[25]

Article 3, Section 1 of the UNCRC could potentially be used by the state to decide your child's reproductive future on issues such as abortion and sterilization, if the decision is believed to be "in the best interest of the child."

Article 13 of the UNCRC is also of importance to homeschoolers. This article states:

> The child shall have the right to freedom of expression: this right shall include freedom to seek, receive and impart information and ideas of all kinds, regardless of frontiers, either orally, in writing or in print, in the form of art, or through any other media of the child's choice.[26]

This article could present a threat to homeschooling parents who are frequently accused of "child neglect" by legislative and social service opponents. Parents could be accused of creating an educational environment that does not allow a child access to information, thereby restricting the child's new rights under the UNCRC.

The statist view of education is furthered by the UNCRC in Article 28, which calls for the state to "take measures" to "encourage regular attendance in schools." Article 29 actually directs the education of the child to develop "respect for human rights . . . and for the principles enshrined in the Charter of the United Nations." Few Christian homeschool settings are going to accomplish this United Nations goal.

Doug Phillips, director of Government Affairs for the National Center for Home Education, writes:

> Rights to freedom of expression, freedom of association, and freedom of religion granted to children by the treaty could easily be construed by a court hostile to home schooling as a justification for requiring that children be examined orally by a school board or social service worker before the state would grant approval on any home schooling request. . . . This procedure would constitute one of the "investigation" techniques required by the treaty to prevent parental infringement on the rights of the child.[27]

The possibility also exists that under the UNCRC, the state would not have to have the permission of the child in question to make decisions on the child's behalf. Because of the child's minor legal status, the state assumes the role of guardian, acting in the child's "best interest," regardless of the child's preferences.

Licensing Parents?

Those who promote the UNCRC frequently cite statistics on child abuse, neglect, juvenile crime, or human rights abuses in the Third World as justification for this treaty. It is interesting to note that this same rationale is being used to promote the idea of state licensing for parents. This concept of state licenses for parenting could provide a framework for the implementation of the UNCRC.

A recent book by Dr. Jack Westman, professor of psychiatry at the University of Wisconsin in Madison, is being hailed by one legal expert as a "Magna Carta for children." His book is entitled *Licensing Parents: Can We Prevent Child Abuse and Neglect?* What once would have been viewed as an Orwellian joke, is now seriously being proposed as a method of controlling child abuse. Westman's book is getting serious attention across the country by those in the judicial branch of government as well as social service groups.

Judge Charles Gill of the superior court, state of Connecticut, writes of Westman's book:

> Unlike many new ideas that are simply trial balloons to test public opinion or reactions without serious forethought, this proposal has solid statistical, factual, and logical support. It is thoroughly researched and convincingly presented. . . . Even the legal community will have to reexamine the status of children in America. Are they people or property? I believe that Dr. Westman heads us in the correct direction on this score as well. He acknowledges that the civil rights children need are not necessarily their legal rights at present. . . . We should be sentenced to seriously examine Dr. Westman's proposal for a new national policy that supports competent parenting.[28]

What is Dr. Westman recommending? Says Westman:

At the level of the states, a national parenting policy could be implemented by licensing parents. By doing so the United States would lead other nations in according civil rights to children and, because few will admit to being against the interests of children, would further enhance respect for human rights in general.[29]

A licensing process for parents would recognize parenting as a relationship sanctioned by society in the same sense that licensing marriage does. . . . It would focus public policies on supporting competent parenting and on remedying or replacing incompetent parenting.[30]

Here is how Westman's licensing idea would work. Westman says that the administration of parent licenses "would be at the level of state and local governments, although enabling federal legislation, such as requiring licenser for the receipt of federal funds, would be helpful in encouraging nationwide consistency."[31] Every parent-to-be would have to apply for a license.

A general parenting license for each mother and father would be granted on meeting the criteria. It would then be validated for each child. . . . If protective services for a child were invoked by actual child abuse or neglect, the license could be placed on probationary status while treatment was ongoing, or it could be suspended during foster placement of the child and treatment of the parent.[32]

What happens to those who refuse a license or who don't qualify for one? Says Westman, "If a mother could not meet licensing standards, child protection laws would be invoked at the time of the child's birth. The custody of the child would be with an agency, and the child's placement would be determined by the circumstances of the situation."[33]

Is Dr. Westman concerned about the violation of parental rights? Not a bit. "The overall importance of protecting innocent children from incompetent parenting justifies the inconvenience to a few parents and the inevitable imperfections of a licensing system."[34]

Dr. Westman's rationale for licensing parents is based on four principles:

1. The human rights principle that all individuals, including children, should be free from abuse and oppression.

2. The civil rights principle that all individuals should have equal access to opportunities to develop their potentials in life.

3. The common good principle in which society has a right to regulate activities that are potentially harmful to others and to society.

4. The humanistic principle that the future success of children as citizens depends upon forming affectionate attachment bonds with their own parents.[35]

Not surprisingly, Dr. Westman is enthusiastic about the United Nations Convention on the Rights of the Child. States Westman:

> The United Nations Convention clearly declares that the state has a role in child-rearing. Because the consent of children is not required for the exercise of parental power, it is in the privacy of their own homes that their civil rights are least assured.[36]

Dr. Westman's contempt for the traditional family and the rights of parents are reminiscent of the words of two long-time children's rights advocates, Ronald and Beatrice Gross, who said,

> Young people are the most oppressed of all minorities. They are discriminated against on the basis of age in every area from movie admissions to sex. They are traditionally the subjects of ridicule, humiliation, and mental torture in homes, schools, and other institutions.[37]

Like radical psychologist Richard Farson, Westman's basic assumption is that the traditional family should be assumed guilty until proven innocent through state licenser. In today's moral, political and legal climate, his idea is catching on.

Selma Sapir is the coordinator of United Nations Affairs for the International Council of Psychologists and she is excited by Jack Westman's ideas.

> As the United Nations prepares for its Global Summit on Social Development

in 1995, one of the most important problems to be discussed is the problem of Social Integration. This book (*Licensing Parents*) is 'must reading' for all persons concerned with ways to eliminate the malaise in our society to find ways to change attitudes and create a healthy climate in all social relationships.[38]

Says David Popenoe, professor of sociology at Rutgers University, "[Westman's book is] a wise and well-researched treatise on why the current generation of children and youth is the first in our nation's history to be less well-off. . . . *Licensing Parents* is an important book for our time."[39]

In late January, 1995, the *Milwaukee Journal* newspaper ran a multi-page article on Westman's book and his idea of licensing parents. The legal and social service experts interviewed on the topic expressed favorable views on the idea. Judge Christopher Foley, a Milwaukee county children's court judge, is also excited by the idea, stating,

I think it's a marvelous idea. Doing the job that I do, you see every day the terrible situations that these children are born into. . . . Licensing is a proposition that's extremely attractive. But I don't believe it is one that is presently feasible from a political standpoint or arguably from a constitutional standpoint.[40]

Not one of the experts interviewed by the *Journal* on this issue expressed strong opposition or concern at the concept of the state's ability to regulate parenting. Like support for the UNCRC, the very real abuse cases across the country are used as a rationale for instituting laws restricting the rights of all people, even the most basic right to bear children, unmolested by the state.

The growing statist world view is evident not only among judges and social workers but among many educators who teach America's public school children. These educators are the cheerleaders for a new paradigm, a new culture where the traditional family has been neutered in its authority, and has actually been replaced by the new state parent, ultimately the United Nations. Education journals continually offer propaganda for presentation to students on the issue of children's rights and the UNCRC.

Ellen Moore, Urgent Action program assistant at Amnesty International in Nederland, Colorado, says,

> Children can be human rights activists, too! . . . When teachers introduce the human rights case of the month, students have an opportunity to put themselves in the victim's shoes as they discuss what is wrong in the situation as outlined in the case sheet and whose human rights are being violated and how. . . . The Children's Edition Urgent Action program can serve as the action component in social studies, civics, religion and ethics, and English classes.[41]

Ellen Moore is describing the prepackaged letter-writing campaigns to various countries about human rights abuses, complete with a prepackaged "fact" sheet from Amnesty International explaining the situation. Moore doesn't address the fact that there are often a variety of views on international conflicts, including causes and effects for various world crises. Her goal is to mobilize students in letter-writing campaigns and to effect political change. Says Moore, "Many teachers have used class letter writing in units on the Bill of Rights comparing and contrasting this document with the Universal Declaration of Human Rights and the United Nations Convention on the Rights of the Child."[42]

The social studies journal *Social Education*, in April/May 1992, even included a sample letter of support for the UNCRC from a high-school student for teachers to use in the classroom. This same issue included a long and detailed listing of children's rights organizations for teachers and students to contact.

The Resistance

Despite the fulsome praise for the UNCRC from some quarters, there is growing opposition on several fronts. Profamily legal analysts have expressed deep concern about the impact of the UNCRC on America's legal landscape. Conservative family advocates, legislators, and broadcasters have begun to outspokenly oppose this treaty's ratification.

Rep. Thomas J. Bliley (R-VA) detailed his views on the dangers of the UNCRC from both the floor of the House of Representatives and in

an op-ed piece in the *Washington Times*. Said
Bliley from the floor of the House:

> The Convention is a fundamentally
> flawed document based on the belief
> that all rights come from government. In
> my opinion, government cannot build
> strong families—only a free people can
> do that. Ratification of the Convention
> would either launch a dangerous assault
> on our system of federalism or embar-
> rass a good many politicians for having
> put faith in a meaningless document. If
> ratified by the United States, the Con-
> vention will do little to improve the
> status of children, will threaten to under-
> mine the rights of parents, and will pro-
> vide a pretext for greater federal intru-
> sion into state and local matters.[43]

Jean Guilfoyle of Human Life International
warns,

> The United Nations Convention on the
> Rights of the Child is a political travesty,
> an invention of mythical rights which
> will deform the child in the attempt to
> transform him/her into a creature of the
> State. Inherent, foundational needs of
> children reside in a strong family and
> community relationships which are free
> from meddlesome political interventions.
> Such relationships must also be free of
> the fracturing influence of State policies
> which seduce children into premature,
> premarital sexual activity, imposing
> drugs, devices and surgeries on the young

in order to satisfy political and economic interests. Responsible government recognizes its responsibilities to the governed but also understands its limitations. The United Nations Convention on the Rights of the Child proposes unlimited practices which are contrary to the principles of good government, are violative of fundamental human dignity and totally unnecessary for the provision of survival needs for the world's children.[44]

The Free Congress Foundation issued a policy statement in 1993 opposing the UNCRC. One of the points raised by the policy statement is the potential impact of the treaty on the issue of abortion.

The Convention on the Rights of the Child, if ratified, may create an across-the-board right to an abortion which would be binding on the United States to the exclusion of any federal or state laws seeking to protect preborn children or women from abortion.

Article 16 states: "No child shall be subjected to arbitrary or unlawful interference with his or her privacy." The U.S. Supreme Court derived the right to abortion from such a right to privacy in *Roe v. Wade* (1973). . . . Could this treaty be a more deceptive, yet even more forceful, way of guaranteeing the right to abortion?

Article 24 (f) establishes the right to "family planning education and services." President Clinton recently rescinded regulations separating abortion from such programs; the children's rights lobby thinks that abortion is a "family planning service."

The policy statement concludes by stating,

The Convention on the Rights of the Child would impose a scheme of children's rights upon American society, trumping any and all federal or state law that got in the way. This scheme erases the family and parental authority from the picture and puts the state in charge of our children. It is fundamentally antagonistic to the tenets of the Declaration of Independence and the Constitution, to the traditions of our country, and to the very concepts of freedom and government on which this nation was founded.[45]

In countries where the UNCRC has been ratified, the states have moved swiftly to enforce the rights given to children and to indoctrinate these children through the schools. In France, for example, a class of nine-year-olds generated the following declaration.

1. Parents do not have unlimited rights over children. They should not speak for us nor make personal decisions for us. . . .

2. All children should have enough to eat but they should not be forced to eat if

they are not hungry. . . . Children have
the right to choose what they want to eat
at home or at school. . . .

3. Children have the right to dress as they
like, to follow fashion and wear their hair
as they like. . . .

4. All children can decide at what point
they cease to be children. If a person
does not feel ready to take responsibilities, he has the right to remain a child.[46]

This "declaration of rights" is anarchy by
children, aided and abetted by the French educational system. America will have to face a
similar onslaught if the UNCRC is ratified by the
United States Senate.

On 16 February 1995, American ambassa-
dor to the United Nations, Madeleine Albright,
signed the U.N. Convention on the Rights of the
Child. This act officially puts the treaty on the
front burner of Bill Clinton's policy making.

As of the writing of this book, the UNCRC
awaits action in the Senate Foreign Relations
Committee, under the new chairmanship of
Sen. Jesse Helms. Helms's leadership on the
foreign Relations Committee is encouraging for
those who oppose the CRC. But the U.N. convention has the outspoken, well-financed support of large education unions, the news media,
many international children's rights groups, and
of course, the United Nations. There is growing
international pressure for the United States to
sign on. The U.S. is the last Western nation that
has not ratified the treaty.

Those who believe this treaty is a threat to the family should contact their U.S. senators. Phone calls and letters are critically important in demonstrating grassroots opposition. Many senators have never read the U.N. convention, or they support it only for pragmatic reasons. After all, who wants to go on record as voting *against* a treaty to help children? We must educate our elected representatives to the dangers of the CRC.

Persons who oppose this measure should commit themselves to educating as many people as possible. Organization and vigilance will be critical to the short-term defeat of the U.N. convention. Vigilance will be necessary because the supporters of the convention have vowed that ultimately the United States *will* sign this treaty. The question of the hour is this: Will American taxpayers show equal resolve to defend their children? In short, whose children are they?

The following organizations and resources are available for further research on the topic of the children's rights movement and the UNCRC.

Parents Information Network (P.I.N.)
P.O. BOX 733
Elm Grove, Wisconsin 53122
(414) 821-1873

P.I.N. is a parents information organization that offers a wide variety of videos, cassette tapes, books, and position papers on the issue of the UNCRC, children's rights and federal education reform, Goals 2000. P.I.N. also offers speakers on these topics for your church, school, or radio/television.

> National Center for Home Education
> P.O. Box 125
> Paeonian Springs, Virginia 22129
> (703) 338-7600

The National Center offers information on a variety of homeschool and parents rights issues. They have created an excellent, well-documented special report on the UNCRC, as well as Action Alert sheets for your church bulletins, school newsletters, etc.

> Family Research Council
> 700 13th Street NW, Suite 500
> Washington, D.C. 20005
> (202) 393-2100

Another profamily watchdog group is the Family Research Council in Washington, D.C. This organization keeps track of any legislation on capital hill that affects the family. They offer a newsletter, "Washington Watch," to keep Christians alert to threats on their freedoms.

> Free Congress Research and Education Foundation
> 717 Second Street NE
> Washington, D.C. 20002
> (202) 546-3000

The Free Congress Foundation is working to keep American freedoms alive and educating taxpayers on issues such as the UNCRC through its Policy Insights papers.

Notes

1. Douglas Phillips, "The United Nations Convention on the Rights of the Child," National Center for Home Education Special Report.

2. Ibid.

3. Nigel Cantwell, "Conventionally Theirs: An Overview of the Origins, Content, and Significance of the Convention on the Rights of the Child," *Social Education* (April/May 1992): 207–210.

4. Richard Farson, *Birthrights: A Bill of Rights for Children* (New York: Macmillan, 1974), jacket cover.

5. Ibid., 9.

6. Ibid., 42–43.

7. Ronald and Beatrice Gross, eds., *The Children's Rights Movement: Overcoming the Oppression of Young People* (Garden City, New York: Anchor Press/Doubleday, 1977): 321–322.

8. Ibid.

9. Doug Phillips, "Action Alert," National Center for Home Education, 1994. Reprinted with permission of the National Center for Home Schooling.

10. Ibid.

11. Stuart Hart, "From Property to Person Status," *American Psychologist* (January 1991): 55.

12. Ibid., 56.

13. Ibid., 57.

14. Michael Jupp, "The International Year of the Child: Ten Years Later" (Academy of Political Science Proceedings, vol. 37) iss. 2 (1989): 44.

15. William Fernekes, "Children's Rights in the Social Studies Curriculum: A Critical Imperative," *Social Education* (April/May 1992): 203–204.

16. Ibid.

17. Beverly Edmonds, "The Convention on the Rights of the Child: A Point of Departure," *Social Education* (April/May 1992): 205–207.

18. Cantwell, "Conventionally Theirs," 209.

19. Ibid.

20. Geraldine Van Bueren, "Autonomy and the Child: The International Education Rights of the Child," *Social Education* (April/May 1992): 215.

21. Ibid.

22. Ibid.

23. Phillips, "The U.N. Convention on the Rights of the Child."

24. From the treaty, The United Nations Convention on the Rights of the Child.

25. Phillips, "The U.N. Convention on the Rights of the Child," 8.

26. From the treaty, The United Nations Convention on the Rights of the Child.

27. Phillips, "The U.N. Convention on the Rights of the Child."

28. Jack Westman, *Licensing Parents: Can We Prevent Child Abuse and Neglect?* (New York Insight Books, 1994): ix. From the introduction by Charles Gill.

29. Ibid., 283.

30. Ibid., 284.

31. Ibid., 240–241.

32. Ibid., 241.

33. Ibid., 242.

34. Ibid., 243.

35. Ibid., 245–246.

36. Ibid., 153.

37. Beatrice and Ronald Gross, eds., *The Children's Rights Movement: Overcoming the Oppression of Young People* (Garden City, New York: Anchor Press/Doubleday, 1977): 1.

38. Westman, *Licensing Parents,* book jacket.

39. Ibid.

40. Lois Blinkhorn, "Should Parents Need Licenses?" *Milwaukee Journal,* 22 January 1995.

41. Ellen V. Moore, "Children Can Be Human Rights Activists Too!," *Social Education* (April/May 1992): 217.

42. Ibid., 218.

43. Congressman Thomas Bliley, Statement from the floor of the House, 17 September 1990.

44. Jean M. Guilfoyle, "U.N. Convention on Rights of Child? Wrong!," *Human Life International Reprint 33.*

45. Susan Hirschmann, "The Coming Children's Rights Invasion," Free Congress Foundation *Policy Insights* Number 503 (February 1993).

46. *Le nouvel Educateur,* Documents no. 213, (February 1990). As quoted in *Social Education* (April/May 1992): 229. Full declaration obtainable from PEMF, BP109, F-06332 Cannes La Bocca Cedex, France.